Visions·From·The·Fields·Of·Merit

Visions · From · The · Fields · Of · Merit

Drawings of Tibet and the Himalayas

by Philip Sugden

edited by
Carole Elchert

with a Statement by His Holiness the Dalai Lama,

a Preface by Carole Elchert,

and a Foreward by Daniel Entin, Executive Director,
the Nicholas Roerich Museum, New York.

Floating Temple Press, USA

ISBN: 0-9672503-0-7

First published in 1999 by
FLOATING TEMPLE PRESS, USA

Library of Congress Cataloging-in-Publication Data.

**This book was underwritten for Floating Temple Press
through the kind generosity of**

Donald and Monica Badertscher, Findlay, Ohio
Robert and Ruth Balcomb, Findlay, Ohio
The Brown-Forman Corporation,
Louisville, Kentucky
Richard and Barbara Deerhake, Findlay, Ohio
George Dewey, Victoria, Texas
Carole Elchert, Findlay, Ohio
Beverly Fisher, Findlay, Ohio
Frank and Nan Guglielmi, Findlay, Ohio
Sonia Gunderson, Fairfield, Iowa
Edwin and Barbara Heminger, Findlay, Ohio
Sandra and Kevin Henning, Findlay, Ohio
Jeff Nichols, Granville, Ohio
W. Michael and Elizabeth Saunders-Linn, Findlay, Ohio
Carl and Zan Palmer, Findlay, Ohio
Dave and Betty Lou Stuber, Fremont, Ohio
Claralice and Carl Wolf, Bluffton, Ohio

For more information about artwork, exhibitions, or books, write to
Floating Temple Press, P.O. Box 572, Findlay, Ohio 45839 USA

Printed by The Courier Commercial Printing,
Findlay, Ohio

Dedication

This book is dedicated to my mother Eve Sugden for her support and love; to Carole Elchert, my devoted companion in the fields of merit; and to the more than one hundred and twenty thousand Tibetans "living in exile who struggle to keep their culture alive and to those still living in Tibet who struggle just to stay alive." -- Excerpt, *White Lotus* --

1. **Tibetan Boy with Indian Army Parade Hat**: Drawn on location at Choglamsar Tibetan Refugee Camp, Ladakh. 1988. Graphite on 16" x 20" archival paper.

In the collection of Edwin and Barbara Heminger, Findlay, Ohio

In 1988, the document on the right was secretly smuggled from Eastern Tibet to Lhasa, where it was carefully slipped into Phil Sugden's pocket while he was sketching in the Potala Palace. Sugden then carried it out of Tibet and delivered it to the Dalai Lama's representative in New Delhi, India, for translation. The representative stated solemnly that if the Chinese police had discovered the identity of the Tibetan who had carried this document to Lhasa, that person may have been sentenced to life in prison or could have been shot without being questioned. Later that same year the translated version was submitted to the United Nations sessions on human rights abuses in China. The following is the translation of the letter:

TO: THE UNITED NATIONS ORGANIZATION

This is our most fervent appeal to you. As is well-known throughout the world, Tibet has a long history of independence. However, China, with its brutal military strength, has swallowed our nation and inflicted heart-rending suffering on our people for more than three decades now. In our suffering, we place our hope on His Holiness the Dalai Lama, who--we hope--will deliver us from our long period of sorrow.

We appeal to the United Nations to take an immediate step for the restoration of our independence based on truth, justice, and history, and to enable His Holiness the Dalai Lama to return to Tibet. Just as many nations have gained their independence in the light of truth and justice, we hope the United Nations will help in the restoration of Tibet's independence too. This appeal is from all the people of Tibet--now suffering due to the loss of independence.

With high regards,

People of Markham, Kham, Tibet

Acknowledgment

I want to express my sincere gratitude to the following people who are responsible, in some way, for helping these images and the writing to find their way into print. I am primarily indebted to Carole Elchert for major technical and creative rewriting and the editing of endless drafts produced by a right-brained visual artist. Her perspiration and inspiration are part of the work in all of its stages; and for several years of editing and her abiding faith, I am sincerely thankful.

I am grateful for the generosity of the underwriters on this project, without whom this book would exist only as an idea. Thank you Don and Monica Badertscher, Robert and Ruth Balcomb, the Brown-Forman Corporation, Richard and Barbara Deerhake, George Dewey, Carole Elchert, Beverly Fisher, Frank and Nan Guglielmi, Sonia Gunderson, Edwin and Barbara Heminger, Sandra and Kevin Henning, Jeff Nichols, W. Michael and Elizabeth Saunders-Linn, Carl and Zan Palmer, Dave and Mary Lou Stuber, Claralice and Carl Wolf--you all have given a dream a path to its completion.

I appreciate the insightful editing by Scott Mulrane, Claralice Wolf, Kathleen Brooks, and Lu Capra; and the proofreading help of my mother Eve Sugden, Susan Burris, Parker Sams, and Mel Veltri. Also, thanks to my friend Edwin Bernbaum of Berkeley, California, for his insightful suggestions. Thanks to Sean Risser, graphic designer, for his creative ideas during the layout process. Endless thanks to Robert Calmus for photographing the artwork and to both him and Laura Calmus for the gourmet dinners. Thanks to Greg Petropoulos for his stimulating conceptual discussions over lunch. I appreciate the unfailing generosity of Illic and Daniela Sirotti for many late nights on the internet and their perennial support. Warm appreciation to dear friends Robert and Martha Bright, who have underwritten the lives of two artists for much longer than the original three-month request. And my appreciation to Daniel Entin, the Executive Director of the Nicholas Roerich Museum in New York, and its staff for their generosity and trust when the museum was turned over to me for a six-month series of exhibitions to celebrate the 1991 International Year of Tibet.

Both Carole Elchert and I thank David Phillips, who in 1987 as Executive Director of the Congressional Human Rights Foundation in Washington, D.C., shared his time, gave essential input on contacts for projects and exhibits, and helped get the *White Lotus* book and video project underway.

I also want to acknowledge the following people and organizations who made our journeys to Tibet and the Himalayas both successful and memorable. Many thanks especially to Zimba Sherpa at Khumbi-Ila Trekking in Kathmandu <zimba@trekking.mos.com.np>, who, along with Dawa Dorje <dawadorj@public.ls.xz.cn>, Suping and Jigme of Tibet International Sports Travel of Lhasa, Tibet, worked tirelessly with the unpredictable circumstances of traveling on the roof of the world. Thanks to Bindu, Sohan, Uttam, and the staff of the Kathmandu Guest House in Kathmandu, Nepal--all of whom have become friends over the years--for their genuine warmth and incomparable Nepali hospitality. And special thanks to my Tibetan brother Pema Rinzing of White Lotus Trekking in Leh, Ladakh, for arranging and guiding our journeys into the restricted regions; and my Nepali brother Ganesh Shanker of Kathmandu for his cherished friendship and support.

The advance purchase of location drawings made four of my journeys to the Himalayas and Tibet possible. Special thanks to those dedicated friends and patrons in Findlay, Ohio, and elsewhere, for years of support and generosity.

Philip Sugden

2. The Kathmandu
   Guest House
   Thamel, Kathmandu, Nepal.
   <kgh@Thamel.mos.com.np>

3. **Kumbum Chorten, Gyantse:** 1987. Sepia ink on 38" x 52" Stonehenge paper.

Images

Image Number

1 Tibetan Boy with Indian Army Parade Hat

2 Kathmandu Guest House

3 Kumbum Chorten, Gyantse, Tibet

4 The Dalai Lama with the Author

5 Author at Pangong Lake, Ladakh

6 Carole Elchert in Southeastern Tibet

7 Author at Rongbuck Monastery, Tibet

8 Gate n. 1. an opening for passage

9 Varanasi, India

10 Author with Nepali Children

11 Catalyst

12 Thyangboche Monastery, Nepal

13 Awakening

14 Cliffs at Lamayuru Monastery, Ladakh

15 Toling Monastery, Western Tibet

16 Annapurna Temple, Bhaktipur, Nepal

17 Fragments from Another World

18 Author with Pema Angyal, Mustang

19 Houses in Lo, Mustang

20 Portrait: Lobsang

21 Portrait: Pilgrim at Rongbuck

22 Curtains at Drigung Monastery, Tibet

23 Jokhang Temple, Lhasa, Tibet

24 Chortens in the Walled City of Lo (Mustang)

25 Inscriptions on Emptiness

26 Garphu Monastery, Upper Mustang

27 Hindu Temple, Kathmandu

28 Nomad Tent, Western Tibet

29 Sakya Monastery, Tibet

30 The Enigmatic Universe at Sakya Monastery

31 Baskets on a Window Ledge, Bhaktipur

32 Leh Palace, Ladakh

33 Hindu Temple and Pipal Tree, Bhaktipur, Nepal

34 The Doors of Perception #3

35 Order out of Chaos #2

Image Number

36 Prayer Wheels at Thyangboche

37 Tibetan Shepherdess

38 House in Tethang, Mustang

39 Farm in Kathmandu Valley

40 Monks in Hemis Monastery, Ladakh

41 Fractured Christ

42 Gate to Lo Mantang (Mustang)

43 John Westmore at Tsaparang, Tibet

44 Sabu Monastery, Ladakh

45 Altar at Samye Monastery, Tibet

46 Three Changtang Landscapes

47 The Wind of Liberation

48 House in Samar, Mustang

49 Nomad Encampment, Western Tibet

50 Manuscripts from a Unified Field

51 Spituk Monastery, Ladakh

52 Soup Cauldrons, Sera Monastery, Tibet

53 Last Dance at Drigung Dundro

54 Birenthanti, Nepal

55 Potala Palace, Tibet

56 Satellite Dishes in Kathmandu

57 The Final Frontier

58 Tidrom Nunnery, Tibet

59 Shrine in Namche Bazar, Nepal

60 Lhasa Rooftops & Jokhang Temple

61 Order out of Chaos #1

62 Entering the Mandala

63 Haystacks in Pokhara, Nepal

64 Relief Sculptures at Chongye

65 Lamayuru Monastery, Ladakh

66 Author drawing in Tibet

67 Holy Man's Cave, Western Tibet

68 Tibetan Mani Stones, Ladakh

69 Tibetan with Prayer Beads

70 Dalai Lama with Elchert and Sugden

4. His Holiness the Dalai Lama with artist Philip Sugden in his
Findlay, Ohio, studio. *Photo: Robert Calmus*

THE DALAI LAMA

MESSAGE

For many centuries the arts have played a major role in the spiritual development of the Tibetan people. Art is an important and fundamental language that has the ability to dissolve borders and transcend the seeming differences between cultures, awakening within us all a sense of our oneness.

Over the years, it has been a pleasure to meet artists, like Philip Sugden and Carole Elchert, who express this understanding in their work. I have known Philip since he and Carole visited Dharamsala in 1988 during the creation of their book and video, *White Lotus: An Introduction to Tibetan Culture*. Since then, I was able to visit their home and Philip's studio in Findlay, Ohio, where I was introduced to his work.

As for the paintings created by the artists of Tibet, they serve as vehicles of spiritual development. In a similar sense, Philip's artwork has been, for him, part of an ongoing pilgrimage, particularly since first meeting Tibetan refugees in Kathmandu in 1978. Based on his journeys to the Himalayas and Tibet, he has created a body of work that testifies to his dedication, not just for the cause of the Tibetan people, but also to the transformation of people through the process of art.

March 31, 1999

Preface

Over the twenty years I have known Philip Sugden, he has been the stalwart artist I am not. He has corralled time in a working studio for artwork, while mustering the willpower to avoid the distractions of a dishwater life. On the trips, his focus is steadfast: converting impressions and insights into drawings on a page. Filling a page and thereby completing a life as an artist--it was simply this activity, which has brought about the developments in his artwork, or as he says, "the transformation in his psyche."

In the routine and discipline of a focused life, we are different as artists. But in the inevitability of transformation, we have both amassed the treasures of being caught up in the artistic process. In my view, it is not a particular thing a person does that confers on him or her the status of "artist" or "artistic." It is a simpler initiation. It is the willingness to step into the stream of our own life, and there the muse waits; the heavens rise from the earth's routine; the darkly mysterious process itself becomes the light with which we discover new forms and the truths of our experiences. I agree with ancient philosophies which say that the material universe is the playground of the mind, and the artistic process is the fertile play.

It cannot be denied that we all are artists in creating a collective world of diverse values and beliefs and a personal world of fictions too, for we are artists who must create as surely as we must breathe. For humans who must breathe and change, art is the most obliging of transformative experiences, and this process Phil describes deftly in the words of his journals and in the remarks on his artwork. For Phil Sugden, producing art and producing a life are ultimately one and the same process. Thus, he remains a willing, joyful captive of the imagination.

Carole Elchert

6. Writer and photographer Carole Elchert on horseback at Basum Tso (Lake),
   Kongpo, Southeastern Tibet.

Foreword

The responsibility is great for the creative artist who attempts to document a civilization that is rapidly being eroded in its everyday reality, and at the same time is increasingly romanticized and idealized in the minds of the general public. In the case of Tibetan culture, the idealizing and romanticizing has created its own mythology, its own established form, for it has been occurring for centuries--the "Shangri-La" factor, if you will. This challenges the artist to weigh the reality and the fantasy (both perhaps true, but different) and to choose carefully the path he will tread in his work. For the artist in such a situation, there is much tightrope walking to do, and his efforts to maintain a clear view must be doubled. He must find a balance between maintaining an objective distance and making his own subjective point of view known.

The responsibility of the artist is even greater when matters of conflict and peace are involved. Because the artist is much more than a craftsman, because the artist has powers of perception and levels of understanding greater than those of the rest of us, it falls to the artist to lead in matters of concern to the world. There is no question that art can be a great force for understanding and for peace, for art can easily transcend the forces of divisiveness and separateness. As a unifier of humanity, art has no equal. Its language knows no borders, its message flows easily and everywhere, like a stream.

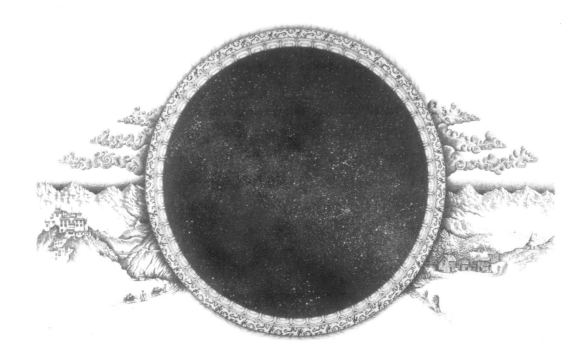

Philip Sugden has traveled to the regions of Tibet, Nepal, and northern India for years. His powers of observation are indeed clear, and his art is put to the service of the highest efforts--to bring information and understanding of the Tibetan plight and the Tibetan cause, and of Tibetan life too. Sugden does this quietly, without trumpeting, without speech-making. Whether he would accept for himself the above mentioned exalted role and responsibility of the artist I cannot know--he is after all an unassuming, modest man--but art has its own ways, its own life, and, once created, fulfills its role nonetheless.

The book you have in hand is an instrument, once created and sent out into the world, that will do much to inform us all about a part of the planet whose reality we know too little about, and explain to us why we must care about it.

Daniel Entin, Executive Director
Nicholas Roerich Museum, New York

Philip Sugden

Philip Sugden formally studied with the contemporary painter, Arnaud D'Hauterives, of Paris. Since graduating from the New York School of Visual Arts and the Paris American *Academie des Beaux Arts et du Langues*, Sugden has made eleven journeys to Himalayan regions, including Ladakh, Mustang, and Tibet.

In 1990, he and writer Carole Elchert were awarded grants from the Ohio Joint Program in the Arts and Humanities and the National Endowment for the Humanities to create an ambience

5. Philip Sugden at Pangong Lake, Ladakh, 1996.
Photo: Carole Elchert

video based on their 1988 Cultural Arts Expedition to the Himalayas and Tibet. As guests of His Holiness the Dalai Lama and the Tibetan Government in Exile, they spent six months in Tibetan communities throughout India, Nepal, Ladakh, and Tibet. The expedition gathered images and recordings for a PBS presentation and the companion book entitled, *White Lotus: An Introduction to Tibetan Culture*, published by Snow Lion. Many of Sugden's studio works and location drawings are included in *White Lotus*.

In 1991, Sugden and Elchert co-organized with The University of Findlay the fourteenth Dalai Lama's speaking engagement at the university, where both are faculty members in the College of Liberal Arts. While in Findlay, the Dalai Lama visited Sugden's studio where he accepted a drawing. Since then, Sugden and Elchert have organized numerous visits and performances of Tibetan monks throughout Ohio.

As guest curator at the Nicholas Roerich Museum in New York, Sugden organized a six-month series of exhibitions, which celebrated the 1991-92 International Year of Tibet. Sugden's artwork has been exhibited internationally in such major cities as New York, London, Paris, Washington, Louisville, Melbourne, and Kathmandu.

As an Assistant Professor of art, he teaches classes in drawing and "Art as a Transformative Experience," as well as team teaching with Carole Elchert a popular honors seminar, "An Introduction to Tibetan Culture." In 1998, ten of his works were exhibited at the Denise Bibro Gallery in New York as part of the "World Artists for Tibet" exhibition series.

Although he lectures nationally on art and Tibetan culture, Sugden spends most of his time in his studio working on a series of large installation-drawings, among other projects.

7. Sugden working at Rongbuck Monastery, Tibet, (Mt. Everest in the background).
   Photo: Carole Elchert

Introduction

by Philip Sugden

"Art...provides the essential language for the affirmation of being...it is the evolving consciousness itself, the mastery of reality by tenuous perception."
Herbert Read, *Icon and Idea*.

Journal entry: June 20, 1995, Ladakh

On the rooftop of a monastery in northern Ladakh, I had almost completed a landscape drawing when an elderly Buddhist monk, who had been quietly watching, leaned toward me and said, "Come. I show you." The wooden steps creaked with age as we descended from the earthen roof into the courtyard.

After entering a side door of the *gompa* (monastery), we climbed another stairway into a hall directly above the main prayer chapel. Walking toward the Yamantaka Chapel, I could barely see the frescoes of wrathful protectors that lined the walls of the dark corridor. As we passed those soot-layered guardians, I caught a glimpse of their bulging, bloodshot eyes and red-stained fangs--too close for comfort.

At the end of the passage the monk swung open a door, drenching the hallway in light, bringing to life the protectors of the *dharma* (Buddha's teachings).

Beyond the door, as light from a wall of windows flooded in, the Yamantaka Chapel exploded with primary and secondary colors. Yamantaka, Conqueror of Death, covered three walls with red, gold, and electric blue. A glossy layer of fresh lacquer intensified the fresco's already powerful effect. Yamantaka's terrifying form had multiple heads draped with skulls, numerous angry eyes, horns, and flames. I stood transfixed by the fresco's massive size.

After a few moments of silence, the monk turned around to face me and announced, "Not real." Pointing to his head he said, "Only here." I smiled and nodded. He pinched my shirt sleeve and turned me around to face the windows. The old monk grinned and pointed out the window at the landscape I had just drawn. "Not real," he proclaimed. Touching his head, he smiled and said, "Only here." Then, while I stared out the window, the monk quietly left the room.

I found the old monk's statement about the mural easy to understand. But he caught me by surprise when he included the rest of the world in this declaration. It was a moment of insight for me that could have been lost had he tried to explain more of the complex philosophy of Tibetan Buddhism.

During the few minutes I was left alone, I found myself staring at the same landscape that I had sketched only a few moments before. From the chapel window, the scene appeared to have taken on a multi-dimensional quality, in contrast to my impression of only ten minutes before from the rooftop which seemed flat, almost black and white. The experience was akin to the difference between viewing a photograph of outer space and actually gazing up at the night sky with a realization of the immense distance between oneself and the stars.

I understood the monk to say that the landscape was an empty plane, like the paper on which I was drawing. And it was on this empty plane, not the paper, that I was creating my reality. This revelation was an obvious paradigm shift, a shift in the way that I perceived my subject matter and everything around me. This insight encouraged me to reconsider not only the creative experience, but the basic significance of my work in general.

Several months after this experience, I spent half a year in my studio working on a large, drawn installation entitled, *Gate: n. 1. an opening for passage.* The image of wrapped figures invites interpretation and allows viewers to be mindful that any significance the work might have is mainly a projection of their own psyches. This drawing was a turning point in my evolution as an artist, because it was the first of my works that did not represent anything outside of itself. Being less illustrative of nature, the piece has more of a capacity to act as a vehicle of nature with a possibility of transforming the viewer.

Although the encounter with the monk was a unique experience, it does not stand alone in a gallery of experiences accumulated on eleven trips to the Himalayas and Tibet. There were other encounters and other events woven together by a thread of similarity, all of which altered the way I viewed and approached my work. I was beginning to realize that the creative process had a cohesive effect on me and the object of my focus, so much so that I began to sense the object's reality and not just my own.

This sense of connection between my notions of self and the actual world around me became more apparent while I sketched on the banks of the Ganges River one morning in 1988. Australian artist John Westmore, writer Carole Elchert, and I made our way through the narrow rows of stalls and temples to the edge of the

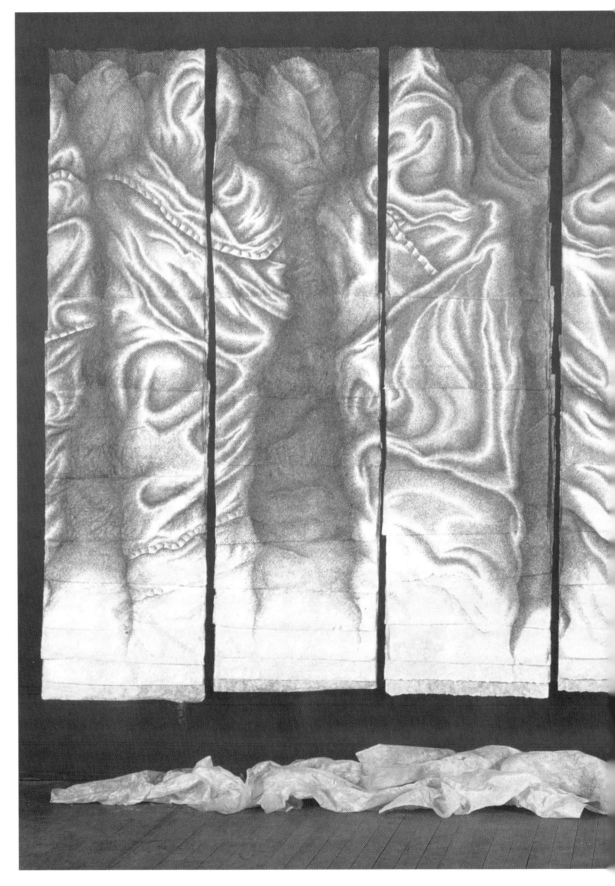

8. **Gate: n. 1. an opening for passage:** Ink on sixty-five sheets of handmade Himalayan Daphne paper. 144" x 84". 1995.

Ganges. The mystical river was shrouded in an early morning fog through which the ghost of a huge orange sun rippled on the eastern horizon. An elderly gentleman in a wooden rowboat ferried us to the sandy shoreline opposite the city.

Journal entry: February 13, 1988, Varanasi, India

A heavy gray mist lifted over the Ganges River, and the wheel of daily life groaned into motion. Ringing prayer bells, honking rickshaws, chanting, bartering, drumming, singing, and crying blended into the holy chaos of Varanasi--the hub of India's spiritual life and the final ground for those souls whose breathless shells the impartial wheel could no longer sustain.

We sat cross-legged on the uncrowded, sandy shoreline of the Mother Ganges, opposite the ancient city of Varanasi. I had almost completed a drawing when I discovered that I could not recall the process. I sat staring, unfocused, at the image on my lap. The seamless rhythm of sounds from the opposite shore had become a mantra that lulled my mind into a kind of silence.

A *saddhu* (holy man), chest-deep in the Ganges, lifted his cupped hands to the sky and poured the infested holy water onto his forehead. A cow defecated at the temple door. A young boy, barely eight, smoked a fat, hand-rolled cigarette. An old woman gently

9. **Varanasi, India:** Drawn on location. 1988. Sepia ink on 11" x 14" archival paper.

placed a leaf of smoldering juniper on the temple steps as an offering. The ashes of cremated flesh were quickly swept from the funeral pyre into the current of the Ganges. Everything is sacrament at the center; all else turns with the wheel and returns to the river.

This experience seemed more enigmatic than the one at the monastery, because I literally "did not recall the process" of physically creating the drawing but was consumed by the sounds and scene around me. I experienced a mild euphoria for some time afterward. In that light-headed state, I found myself projecting less onto the scene around me, feeling less juxtaposed to an alien culture and more attuned to the moment. But like the encounter with the monk, the experience at the river helped to develop within me a sense of relationship with the environment. And, in both cases, it was a perceptual shift that initiated this sense of connection.

Because of the actual circumstances around these experiences, I discovered that the environment itself is a catalyst to perceptual change. In the Himalayas and Tibet the creative experience is charged with a peculiar energy, partly by the fact that I project some mystical significance onto the environment. Even more so, in Central Asia the subject matter specifically and the geography in general are very conducive to having creative, spiritual experiences. These epiphanies could happen while I work in the studio, but, unlike in the studio, experiences on location in Asia awaken my senses, which are usually dulled by the comfort and convenience I seek at home.

In the Himalayas and on the Tibetan Plateau, I was confronted in a profound way with the mysterious quality of being alive. The character of this experience endured amidst my incessant preoccupation with the physical discomforts and the local belief systems which promote the Buddhist concept that all things, by their nature, are empty. The effect was a physiological experience that made it difficult to deny my relationship, not just with the

10. Sherpa children pose for a photo while Sugden draws in the Himalayan village of Thame, Nepal. *Photo: Carole Elchert*

environment but with emptiness as well. For me, emptiness is a meeting point between my awareness of self and the environment. This might better be understood through an analogy with visual arts. In order to create a cohesive, balanced composition, an artist must be as aware of the empty space on the picture plane as the positive shapes being drawn.

The notion that the environment itself can act as a catalyst for a perceptual change became more apparent to me during a stay at Thyangboche Monastery in the Himalayas. An experience there was the inspiration for a large work produced in the studio several months later entitled, *Catalyst: n. 1. an energy that modifies and especially increases the rate of another energy without being consumed in the process.* This installation-drawing explores the concept of emptiness and relationship. The following is the journal entry from that day at the monastery:

Journal entry: April 10, 1987, Thyangboche Monastery, Nepal

Early this morning, while the sun faintly lit the sky behind the snow-covered peaks of the Himalayas, a monk climbed a ladder into a room overlooking the monastery's front courtyard. To wake the other monks, he beat on a steel oxygen cylinder, a memento from an Everest expedition years before. Half an hour later, he returned to summon the monks to morning prayer by blowing into a conch shell. Its deep tone returned as a haunting echo from the walls of mountains that closely surround Thyangboche Monastery.

By the time I crawled out of my sleeping bag, some of the younger

11. **Catalyst: n. 1. an energy that modifies and especially increases the rate of another energy without being consumed in the process.** Ink on 48" x 96" handmade Himalayan Daphne paper, Tibetan prayer flag, plexiglass, steel rod.

monks had already trudged up the ridge in front of the cloister, carrying bundles of prayer flags on bamboo poles along with other Buddhist paraphernalia. These trappings were used to construct a small altar on a stone shrine hundreds of feet above Thyangboche. Before I had finished drinking tea, the young monks, who were high above the monastery, began blowing the large *dunchen* (horns), which sent out deep groans that sounded like phantom whales from the ancient Sea of Tethys. I dressed in my warmest parka and ascended the ridge with several of the older monks and the monastery's lama. The wind was unsympathetic to the devotion paid by the Buddhist monks as they offered piety to emptiness in their annual Lhasing Ceremony.

The monks, wrapped in woolen robes, sat cross-legged in a single line, facing the stone shrine. Behind them stood a row of tall rhododendrons--the foreground to a ridge that rose up to the sacred peak of Ama Dablam. In front of each monk a bench-like table held a prayer book and a cup of hot buttered salt tea. On the edge of the reliquary, an altar was created using seven brass water bowls, several silver goblets, colorful butter sculptures, incense, two *thangka* (scroll) paintings--one a protector thangka, the other of the much

12. **Thyangboche Monastery and Mt. Ama Dablam, Solu Khumbu, Nepal:** Drawn on location.
1983. Sepia ink on 11" x 14" archival paper.

In the collection of Jean Graham, Beaver Creek, Colorado

venerated Guru Rinpoche--and a bowl of *kapsay* (crackers).

Behind the shrine, the ridge slopes into a gully of boulders several hundred feet below. A constant wind howled from the gorge, and the sweet scent from a smoldering mound of juniper branches next to the shrine was drawn into the atmosphere. A monk climbed the earth-covered monument and, leaning into the wind, securely planted all of the bamboo poles. The muslin flags snapped, and the poles strained against the strong wind of the Himalayas, sweeping the wood-block printed prayers into the Buddhist void. The stage was set for a profound drama, a primordial encounter between a person's sense of relationship with the earth and the emptiness described in Buddhist thought.

Razor-edged snow peaks cut through a layer of clouds as monks sang prayers in monotone, slowly increasing in volume and intensity. An unintentional harmony developed between the deeper drones of the older monks and the higher-pitched tones of the younger adepts. The harmonies created an irresistible spell against an orchestra of snapping prayer flags, cawing crows, and whipping wind across the ridge.

With eyes closed, sitting cross-legged near the monks, I found myself spontaneously swaying back and forth with the rhythm of the chant. The intermittent crashes of cymbals, ringing

bells, blasting horns, and thundering
monastic drums filled the rarefied air
with so much distracting sound that
we were startled from our meditative
trances. There were moments of for-
getfulness, lightness that compelled
me to open my eyes for the reassur-
ance that there was still a difference
between me and the sounds.

For the rest of that afternoon I sat in the sun in front of the
monastery, lucid, scribbling in my sketch book impressions that
remained in my visual memory from the previous four hours.
For me, the ceremony was a performance-art, a liturgy, and a rite
that provided emptiness with a medium through which to take
form.

After experiences such as these, I am convinced that art has
existed as liturgy, as a vehicle for transformation for thousands of
years in tribal cultures. In those traditions artists are shamans
and priests who, through their refined vision, act as intermediaries
between the known and the unknown. The intent of their work,
broadly speaking, is the transformation of the individual from an
unconscious observer to that of a conscious participant. For the
Australian aborigine, the Tibetan, the Hopi, and the animistic
tribes around the globe, art is the language of interconnection,
linking the limited sensual knowledge of the world to the vast,
invisible reality of the universe. Even in our modern technological
culture, it is my opinion that all we create and all we are is
animistic, that is, we seek in our art and belief systems this
connection to the earth, the universe, and the unknown.

Even though I believe this about art, you would think that after
twenty-five years as an artist and eleven journeys to the Himalayas
and Tibet, I would have developed a better understanding of art
in particular and of my relationship to the universe in general. It
seems that the more I explore through the creative process, the
more I discover that I know little about myself and almost nothing
about anything else. And it is difficult to take most acquired

knowledge too seriously when, with each new discovery, there is a swell of new questions to answer.

What I do know is that I have experiences and ideas that find their way into imagery. I work and rework images, explore and re-explore ideas. And I return to the Himalayas every so often to experience and re-experience.

And so let me end with one of Carole Elchert's journal entries as she explains the process as it has transpired for me:

During these journeys, Phil explores his creativity but discovers a more fundamental process. As is true for all of us, consciousness pursues him each moment, trying to re-establish itself as the center of his awareness--the mind literally trying to become aware of the mind, of its own nature, as the Buddhists describe the ultimate goal of their practices.

On these trips and in his studio, the more Phil explores artistic expression and the creative process, the more he directly experiences the most basic concepts embedded in Buddhist and Hindu philosophies. Often we have talked about a center to our circling thoughts; the Hindus call it Bindu. There, order already exists, is able to be achieved without the usual compulsion we have as humans to look for and to create order out of the seeming chaos that surrounds us. But looking is essential for artists--that is obvious. It is even more critical for all of us as humans. By looking at chaos, we may have the uncanny insight that the mind has always been looking at the products of the mind and not reality. Perhaps it is when this insight is achieved that the center is reached, the mind is settled, the viewer has become the view.

Phil's life shows that the creative act can be a pilgrimage to the sacred center, the Bindu. Over the years, the studio has become his monastery, and the creative process has become his practice. Each day he tries simply to awaken to a cosmos that already exists beyond the shifting paradigms, the playful projections of his own mind.

(Previous page)

13. **Preliminary Study for Awakening:** Graphite on 72" x 36" treated brown paper.

The image shows a Tibetan nomad with a prayer wheel and rosary in hand, floating slightly off the ground in an awakened or blissful state.

This work was designed as a tribute to the Tibetan people who are enduring repression in their occupied homeland under Chinese military control. In this world of wars and genocide fed by greed and power, it is by cultivating compassion that a people, like the Tibetans, are able to overcome their greatest enemy. As for the Chinese government, they have yet to confront their greatest enemy, which is the same enemy for all mankind, ignorance.

In the collection of Barbara Chapa, Findlay, Ohio

14. **Cliffs below Lamayuru Monastery, Ladakh:** Drawn on location. 1994. Sepia ink on 11" x 14" archival paper.

As I wandered through the narrow paths of the village, I failed, at first, to notice the monastic walls precariously suspended over the edge of the cliff high above me. After shooting a few photographs and viewing the scene through a wide-angle lens, which always exaggerates the angles, I decided to create this sheer perspective of the cliffs. It has become a habit to look through my Nikon F-3 high-point viewfinder for interesting compositions. Three-point perspective in drawings such as this and "Curtains at Drigung" usually offers a more dramatic portrayal of the subject.

Along with the steep angle, I've slightly exaggerated the use of value and directional lines to help capture more of the inward and upward movement of the rock face.

15. **Toling Monastery, Western Tibet:** Drawn on location. 1996.
Sepia ink on 11" x 14" archival paper.

Toling and nearby Tsaparang Monasteries caught my attention because artists Lama Anagarika Govinda and his wife Anila Li Gotami spent months here, just prior to the invasion by the Chinese Red Army, tracing and photographing the frescoes. They knew that the artwork would be destroyed.

The wall is covered with what appears to be pick-ax holes. The Tibetans, during the Cultural Revolution, were forced at gunpoint to destroy their own religious artwork.

Painter John Westmore and I frustrated the Chinese policeman who was there to make sure we did not photograph inside the main chapels where the abuse was still visible. However, he did not stop us from drawing or painting the destruction.

This drawing shows a front view of the ravaged monastery. You can see a lighter area in the center of the wall where a two-story statue of Buddha once stood in the main chapel, which is now missing its roof.

RUINS OF TOLING MONASTERY
WESTERN TIBET

P. Snyder 95

Annapurna Temple
Bhaktipur, Nepal
on location

P. Snyder 78

16. **Annapurna Temple, Bhaktipur, Nepal:** Drawn on location. 1998. Sepia ink on 11" x 14" archival paper.

After returning from Mustang in 1998, I sketched here for an hour with my friend Oscar Hijuelos. Over the years that I have drawn this particular temple, which is dedicated to Annapurna, I have noticed that the homes have slowly encroached upon its sacred space, making it difficult to find a view for drawing.

Of all the temples and trees that I have drawn in the Kathmandu valley, this one holds a special place in my heart. It was the first temple I drew during an earlier trip and was an image used in one of the first large layered paper works.

As best as I can figure, seeds become wedged in the stones of these temples and take root quickly during the daily summer monsoon rains. The Hindu villagers allow the pipal trees to grow on the temples as a sign of respect to nature, a tradition that may be rooted in ancient animistic beliefs. Perhaps they just accept the organic process, whereby the growth forces the stones apart, yet the roots hold and preserve the temple.

There is also a wonderful aesthetic that exists when the organic shapes of the roots intertwine with the more geometric shapes of the man-made structure. And perhaps it is this perceived aesthetic that provokes wonder and gives symbolic meaning to the organic marriage of the tree and the temple.

In the collection of Walt Bovaird, Findlay, Ohio

17. **Fragments from Another World:** Sepia ink on 60" x 30" handmade Himalayan Daphne paper. 1990.

The idea of the temple floating on an island occurred to me during my first trip to the Himalayas in 1978. The temple and tree was an image that stayed in my visual memory, a "fragment" that I carried home with me.

I began layering the papers when I became interested in Tibetan Buddhist prayer flags and the idea that prayers are transported by the wind heavenward, which to Buddhists is emptiness. These wood-block printed muslin flags tend to get bundled and layered as pilgrims tie each new flag to the others.

In the collection of the Brown-Forman Corporation. Louisville, Kentucky

18. Sugden and Pema Angyal, Lo Mantang, Mustang.
   Photo: Carole Elchert

19. **Homes in Lo Mantang, Mustang:** Drawn on location. 1998.
   Sepia ink on 11" x 14" archival paper.

Just after we had settled into camp, next to the main entrance of the walled city, I met a fourteen-year-old boy, Pema, who became my assistant during our stay. I showed him the completed drawings in my sketchbook, which gave him an idea of the subjects I prefer to draw. He knew everyone in town and was able to guide me through the narrow pathways within Lo, leading me to sites that I may never have found on my own. We wandered into homes, climbed onto rooftops, and mounted the wall itself, on which we were able to walk halfway around the city.

Every morning, Pema would put my bag over his shoulder before we began exploring. Once we found a spot, he would clip open my sketchbook, unscrew the cap of my pen, then hand them to me. In the afternoons when classes ended, he was able to keep groups of school children from bothering me while I sat cross-legged on the ground to sketch.

HOMES IN THE
WALLS OF LO-
MANTANG.
MUSTANG.
P. Sugden. 98

20. **Lobsang, a Tibetan Refugee:** Drawn on location at Choglamsar Tibetan Refugee Camp, Ladakh. 1988. Graphite on 8" x 10" archival paper.

Over a period of days, we had been photographing the building of a traditional mud-brick house at Choglamsar. During that time our faces became familiar to the laborers and their faces familiar to us. Several of the men and women had wonderfully lined faces that I wished to draw.

One afternoon, after construction had finished for the day, we went to the home of Lobsang, one of the laborers, and asked him if we could begin pencil and pastel portraits of him. Perhaps because he was aware that we were working on a project that involved the Dalai Lama, he just smiled, sat down, rosary in hand, climbing goggles on his face, lifted his chin, and quietly posed.

In the collection of Kim and Duane Wires, Findlay, Ohio

21. **Tibetan Pilgrim at Rongbuck Monastery, Tibet:** Drawn on location. 1988. Graphite on 8" x 10" archival paper.

We were spending a few days at Rongbuck, one of the highest monasteries on earth, near the northern base of Mt. Everest. Since it is very remote and isolated, we were surprised one morning to see two elderly women wander in. They were pilgrims, having walked hundreds of miles throughout Central Tibet to the temples, monasteries, and nunneries.

We spent some time talking to them as they rested against the walls of an old monastic building, now in ruins. This gave me a few minutes to begin a quick line study. I was able to complete the portrait in the monastery guest house that evening.

In the collection of Kim and Duane Wires, Findlay, Ohio

22. **Curtains at Drigung Monastery, Central Tibet:** Drawn on location. 1991. Sepia ink on 11" x 14" archival paper.

Hanging in the front of the Assembly Hall are curtains of woven yak hair, the material used by nomads to weave their tents. These heavy black curtains absorb heat while keeping out the wind and dust. I was particularly fascinated by the movement of the folds and looked forward to building up the value (shading) to create a sense of the gravity and weight of this wall of curtains.

I discovered this perspective by looking at the outside corner of the main prayer chapel through a 24 mm lens on my camera. The angle offered a novel view of the architecture that seemingly abstracts the forms and tends to give an aura of majesty to the monastery.

23. **Tibetan Pilgrims and the Jokhang Temple, Lhasa, Tibet:**
Drawn on location. 1988. Sepia ink on 11" x 14" archival paper.

The Jokhang Temple, a bustling pilgrimage site and market place, which is Lhasa's spiritual center, was an impossible place to draw. I was surrounded by pilgrims, particularly Khampas, the "warriors" from the East.

Once I started to show them other sketches in the book, I could no longer get any work done. The crowd grew larger, leaving me no choice but to return later to finish the drawing.

Because of the movement around me, I worked in a quick gestural manner and decided to do no more than a contour line drawing without shading, the crowd having won out in the final decision.

In the collection of Oscar Hijuelos, New York

24. **Chortens in the Walled City of Lo, Mustang:** Drawn on
    location. 1998. Sepia ink on 11" x 14" archival paper.

Pema, a self-appointed assistant, and I sat quietly in
the corner of a narrow path viewing these Buddhist
shrines in Lo, the capital of Mustang. While I drew, a
woman came out of her home and down the steps
shown on the left of the drawing. She asked Pema what
I was doing and then went off to wash her hair at the
local water tap. Later, when she returned, her hair rolled
up in a towel, she looked at the nearly completed
drawing and told Pema that I was painting a thangka
(a Buddhist scroll painting that monks usually create
for ceremony or ritual at the monastery). Pema giggled
and, to avoid getting into a long explanation, agreed
with her.

BUDDHIST
SHRINES IN
THE WALLS
OF LO MANTANG
MUSTANG

25. **Inscriptions on Emptiness:** 1994. Sepia ink on 37" x 48" handmade Himalayan Daphne paper.

This work, layered like Tibetan prayer flags, has as a background a Tibetan Buddhist prayer, *om mani padme hum*, which translated means, "praise to the jewel in the middle of the lotus blossom." The prayers fade near the lower half of the work as if the wind had carried them off into Buddhist emptiness. Usually on Tibetan prayer flags an image of a horse represents the wind, but in this work, a Tibetan woman in nomadic dress floats in an awakened state of bliss--arms open to express her ecstasy.

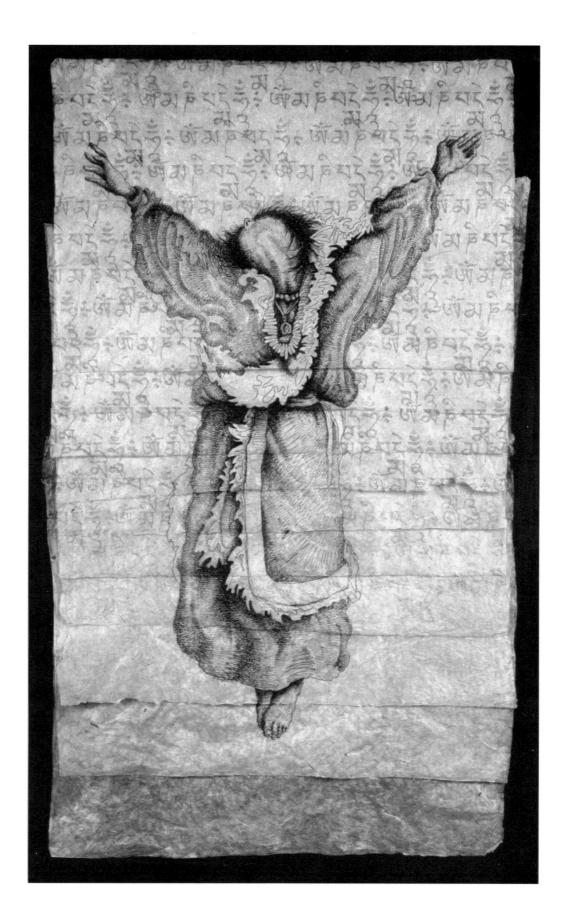

26. **Garphu Monastery, Upper Mustang:** Drawn on location. 1998. Sepia ink on 11" x 14" archival paper.

This monastery, only a few kilometers from the Tibetan border, is built into the sandstone walls of the textured cliff behind it. Monasteries and shrines have always intrigued me as subjects for drawings, because they are reminders of our deeper natures, which we seek to understand in life.

When I sit quietly outside or inside the monastery during a prayer ceremony, concentrating on angles, negative space, textures, and values, I also seem to contemplate my own understanding, or lack of it.

In the collection of Ron Rejmaniak, Houston, Texas

27. **Hindu Temple, Kathmandu:** Drawn on location. 1986.
    Sepia ink on 11" x 14" archival paper.

I sat on the edge of the Jamuna River one morning to draw. Local women brought their morning offerings--a handful of rice and incense on a Banyan leaf--and then left the temple. While I sketched, a body was being cremated only yards away from the temple on a slab of stone next to the river.

A young Nepali man sat quietly beside me while I worked. When I was nearly finished, he introduced himself as Ganesh Shanker and told me that he too painted pictures. Later we went to his home, a thatch-roofed house on the road to Swayambhu Temple, where I met his family and viewed his beautiful traditional paintings. We have considered ourselves brothers ever since.

In the collection of Pauline Hixson

28. **Nomads' Yak Hair Tent, Western Tibet:** Drawn on location. 1996. Sepia ink on 11" x 14" archival paper.

Watching our drivers and the nomads speak at the same time but point in different directions was entertaining, particularly since there are no roads to speak of in western Tibet. We also traded some of our petrol for goat curd, which was a joke on us, because the curd was distastefully sour.

During our short stay with the family, it started to rain, so I sat in our vehicle with the door open and began this drawing. The woven yak hair tent sagged as the rain poured down, which gave me the idea to exaggerate textures and value in the drawing.

29. **Sakya Monastery, Central Tibet:** Drawn on location.
1988. Sepia ink on 11" x 14" archival paper.

Even since my first visit to Sakya in 1986, it has been a special place for me to draw. Although Sakya is one of the poorest towns in contemporary Tibet, as well as one of the most oppressed because of a large contingent of Chinese soldiers, the ancient architecture with its deeply textured walls still exudes a long and powerful history that precedes the Mongol empire.

To draw, I had to stand, leaning against a mud-brick wall. It didn't take long for a rumpled gang of children to gather around to watch me "write a photo," as they describe drawing in Tibetan. They climbed the wall behind me and hung over my shoulders--giggling, playing games, and teasing me. These children were dressed in brown and gray rags and, as I was told, had no school to go to.

I did variations of this drawing on future trips and used them as preliminary studies for several large studio works.

In the collection of Edwin and Barbara Heminger, Findlay, Ohio

(following pages)

30. **The Enigmatic Universe at Sakya Monastery:** Sepia ink and gouache on 84" x 36" handmade Himalayan Daphne paper.

This image is based on location sketches of Sakya Monastery in Central Tibet. Attached to the monastery door is the quote, "Welcome to the theater of the absurd. Price of admission, your mind," from the novel *Steppenwolf* by Herman Hesse. For me, entering the theater is a metaphor for confronting our personal demons.

In the collection of Kevin and Sandra Henning, Findlay, Ohio

31. **Baskets on a Window Ledge, Bhaktipur, Nepal:** Drawn on location. 1983. Sepia ink on 11" x 14" archival paper.

This window is typical of scenes in the older sections of Kathmandu and Bhaktipur. John Westmore and I stood in a narrow street to draw while two women carried on a conversation from their second floor windows--apparently trying to figure out what we were doing.

That year at an exhibition of our drawings in Kathmandu, an older Nepali man commented on this drawing, saying that I was able to see beauty in everyday objects that they normally would not look at twice. I valued that comment since it came from a Nepali and reflected the circularity of mutual appreciation.

In the collection of Jerry and Kathy Vossler, Findlay, Ohio

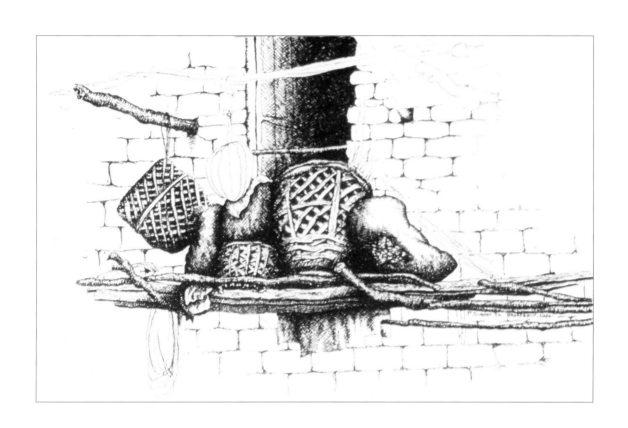

32. **Shrines at Leh Palace, Ladakh:** Drawn on location. 1996.
Sepia ink on 11" x 14" archival paper.

Leh Palace, an impressive sight that dominates the northern landscape, includes a large complex of chapels and shrines built on the side of a steep mountain that overlooks the town of Leh. The side of this mountain is so steep that the only workable view of the buildings is from below. After the drawing was completed, I realized that it was this view that created the imposing scale of the palace complex.

The Russian artist Nicholas Roerich and his expedition spent the summer and autumn of 1925 on the eighth floor of the palace. In his journal, he wrote that the wind caused the building to sway, knocking down a wall in the room that he and his wife were occupying at the time.

In this work, I implied an atmospheric quality by lightly drawing the palace to move it back in the picture plane, thereby allowing the shrines to become more dominant.

LEH MONASTERY
LADAKH

33. **Hindu Temple and Pipal Tree, Bhaktipur, Nepal:** Drawn on location. 1995. Sepia ink on 11" x 14" archival paper.

More than any other subject, I am amazed by the small Hindu temples that over the years withstand the massive weight of ancient pipal trees, which cling to their stone walls. For me, these structures are living monuments whose physical forms bind our fragile beliefs together with the durable truths of nature. They are a marriage of the frail human ideas about the cosmos with the spontaneous and dynamic forces of the universe. I feel reassured that there is balance in the seeming dichotomy of thought and nature.

I've completed many drawings of trees growing on temples and have used this more often than any other motif in preliminary studies for large studio works.

In the collection of Deborah Bays, Lima, Ohio

Tree Temple
Bhaktapur, N.

34. **The Doors of Perception #3:** Sepia ink and gouache on handmade Himalayan Daphne paper.

Artists generally get only a few exceptional ideas during their lives and then create variations on that theme. For me, the tree and temple have been a recurring motif in my work. To cultivate new understanding in the viewer, I explore various ways of handling the image: more innovative formats, different perspectives, or even additional imagery, such as the sleeping man and the monkey.

With each version, the motif of outer space--another reoccurring theme--seems to find its way deeper into the structure, flowing beyond the doorway or window, consuming the stone work of the temple. One day, perhaps, someone will find on my easel a large image of outer space without a trace of the temple or the tree, and I will not be found... anywhere.

In the collection of Jim and Anna Miller, North Baltimore, Ohio

35. **Order out of Chaos #2:** 1996. Sepia ink and gouache on
90" x 72" Mexican Bark paper.

Creating order out of chaos is what artists are trying to accomplish in one sense or another, on one level or another. But it is when viewing a work of art that an essential order can be discovered, a more subtle order that exists within the viewers themselves rather than in the drawing. On the surface of this drawing, an obvious order is created by the elements of composition (balance, rhythm, etc.) which draw together the fragments of paper.

Within the work itself, the man--a symbol of humanity--is sleeping by the door while a monkey sits high in the tree, staring out at the viewer, knowingly. The door is there; it is open, and even the monkey (the divine joker) knows this.

After beginning the drawing on Mexican bark paper, I discovered that I could use some of its natural markings to dictate the shapes and textures of the tree, allowing existing patterns in the paper to become knots or twists in the roots and trunk. In other areas, the natural lines of the bark paper have guided my pen, fashioning some of the tree limbs as they move out and away from the temple.

In the collection of the Brown-Forman Corporation,
Louisville, Kentucky

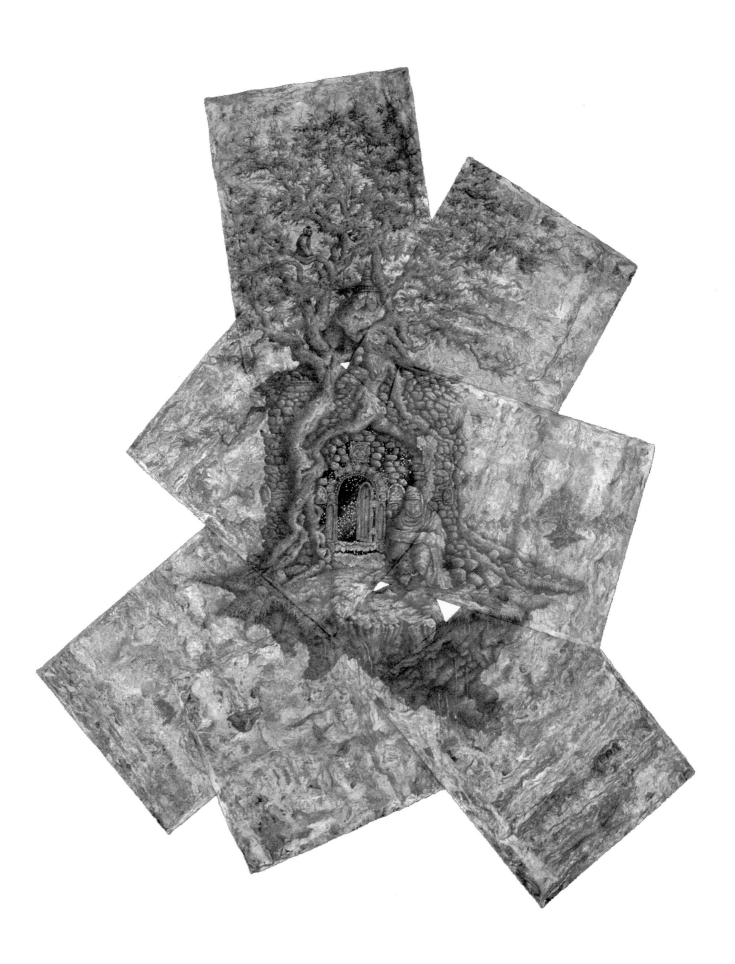

36. **Prayer Wheels, Thyangboche Monastery, Solu Khumbu, Nepal:** Drawn on location. 1988. Sepia ink on 11" x 14" archival paper.

Tinley Sherpa, our friend and a monk at Thyangboche, sat beside me in the courtyard of the monastery while I drew. Tinley is the monastery's artist-in-residence; he paints religious thangkas (scroll paintings) and woodblock prints. I remember that we spent a morning discussing the fundamental difference between Buddhist art, with its aim of spiritual development, and the artwork created in the West for material success.

In the collection of Ken Kamler, New York

37. **Tibetan Shepherdess:** Drawn on location at Choglamsar
Tibetan Camp, Ladakh. 1988. Graphite on 16" x 20"
archival paper.

This shepherdess passed our little guest house
every morning and evening with her sheep, and
every evening Carole spoke with her. She readily
agreed to let me photograph and Carole record as
she hooted and whistled at her sheep. She told us
that the sheep are an honorary herd, given to the
Dalai Lama.

I started this sketch as a gesture drawing and
completed it later in the studio, using the
photographs as reference. Since I use line instead of
washes in the work, I find it easy to draw people,
such as the shepherdess, whose deeply weathered
faces mark the difficult and sad recent history of
Tibet.

It is nearly impossible to convince Tibetans to
pose because they are working and constantly
moving. But in Choglamsar, there are a large number
of refugees who lost their families over the years
since China has occupied Tibet. They know they
are the lucky ones who escaped and are happy to sit
for a portrait while spinning their prayer wheels and
reciting mantras continuously for the people who
remain in Tibet.

In the collection of William Holloway, Wheeling, West Virginia

38. **House at Tethang, Mustang:** Drawn on location. 1998.
    Sepia ink on 11" x 14" archival paper.

This drawing shows the typical architecture of Mustang homes with wood for fuel piled on the roof. Tethang was the poorest and most abject village that we camped near. As we wandered through this fortress-like village, we gathered about ten rag-tag children who happily guided us through the narrow streets that tunneled and wound through the village.

It was difficult to work there because of the number of children who squeezed around us. I could only get a quick gestural drawing started and had to complete this piece later from slides that Carole Elchert had taken.

House at Tethang
Mustang, Nepal
P. Sugden 98

39. **Farm in Kathmandu Valley:** Drawn on location. 1988.
   Sepia ink on 11" x 14" archival paper.

During my earliest visits to Nepal in 1978 and 1979, we could walk for miles across the open fields and irrigation ditches of the Kathmandu Valley. That was part of the mystique of Kathmandu, which draws me back time after time.

This drawing of a typical small farm house captures that quiet time in the valley before 1980. The background shows Swayambhunath, an ancient Buddhist monastery and Hindu temple complex.

In the collection of Jock and Margaret Maynard, Toronto, Canada

40. **Monks in Hemis Monastery, Ladakh:** Drawn on location. 1988. Sepia ink on 8" x 10" archival paper.

These sketches took me less than a minute each to draw while artist John Westmore and I worked inside the prayer hall of Hemis Monastery. The monks were dressing themselves in costumes to dance in the courtyard festival. Not only was it too dark to see any detail inside the hall, but the monks were hurrying as they dressed themselves for the next performance.

In the bright sunlight outside, thousands of people huddled in the courtyard to watch the dances while we had the advantage of being behind the scenes and seeing preparations.

Quick gestural statements were the only option under those conditions. In terms of the creative process, I much prefer the gestural technique. Gesture drawings are less about representing nature and more about recording movement and feelings.

41. **Fractured Christ:** 1997. Sepia ink on 90" x 110" handmade Himalayan Daphne paper.

This work began as a project for a series of exhibitions in New York sponsored by the World Artists For Tibet, who were protesting China's human rights policies toward the Tibetan people.

In Tibet over the last 40 years, more than 1.2 million innocent men, women, and children have died as a result of China's occupation and the Cultural Revolution fanaticism. Over 6 million Tibetans now live without personal and political freedom in their own land. More than 120,000 have escaped the horror by fleeing into exile, and daily, more continue to make the perilous trip across the Himalayas to become refugees in India or Nepal.

However, as this drawing took shape, a conflict arose in my mind. How could I condemn the Chinese for forty years of genocide, imprisonment, and destruction when we have a 200-year history of doing the same to the Native Americans of this country? Our government, along with others in the world community, undermines the Tibetans' call for human rights by allowing the Chinese to commit genocide in the Tibet Autonomous Region, and elsewhere. As long as China's markets are open and trade continues, Tibetan sovereignty and fundamental rights are ignored by most nations.

The crucifixion is one of the Western world's most powerful images, and one of the many forms of torture used by the Red Guard during the Cultural Revolution. I decided to use this symbol as a statement about our responsibility for every human on this planet and as a question that asks, who are we still willing to crucify.

Unlike the Christian cross with the Christ figure, this image shows a woman wearing a rosary, talisman box, and sea shells around her neck, all of which may identify her as a Tibetan Buddhist. The background is the repetitive prayer that most Tibetans chant to gain spiritual merit, and, more importantly, to invoke the blessings of Chenrezig, the god of compassion, for all forms of life in the universe.

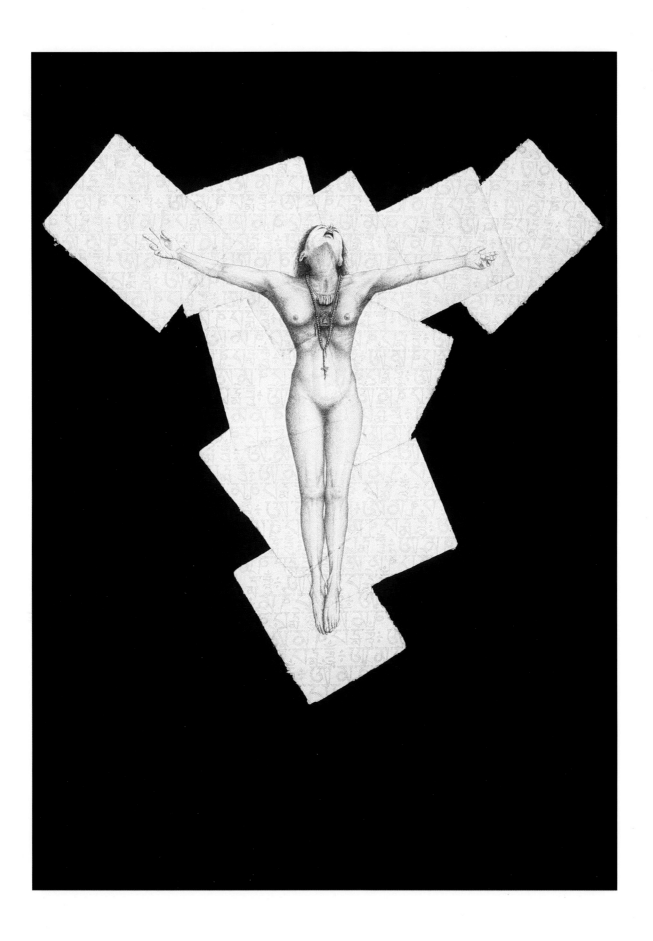

42. **Main Entrance into the Walled City of Lo:** Drawn on
location. 1998. Sepia ink on 11" x 14" archival paper.

My young assistant, Pema, and I sat on the side
of a large *stupa* (shrine) for this view of the northern
entrance into Lo, the capital of Mustang. As I sat
drawing, herders and traders walked by and asked
Pema what I was doing, and he would explain the
drawings to them. In a few cases they asked to see
some of the other drawings in the sketchbook.

One man we met had just walked from Tibet,
carrying a heavy load of canned goods, including
pineapple and Spam, in a basket on his back. Then
he sold this food from Lhasa to the tea shops of Lo.
By spending several hours drawing in one spot, I've
been able to meet the people of the Himalayas, like
this man, and learn more about their daily lives.

This drawing shows one of the three monasteries
in Lo; the palace of the King of Mustang is directly
behind the shrine.

In the collection of William Hale, Lawrence, Kansas

WALL, PALACE, AND
MONASTERY AT
LOMANTANG,
MUSTANG

43. Australian artist, John Westmore, painting at Tsaparang
   Monastery, Western Tibet.

44. **Sabu Monastery, Ladakh:** Drawn on location. 1993.
   Sepia ink on 11" x 14" archival paper.

For me and Australian painter John Westmore,
who is often a traveling companion, this was one of
the quietest, most pastoral settings where we had
ever worked. At 12,000 feet above sea level, we
looked over vast distances of the Changtang plateau,
as well as the Indus River and two mountain ranges.
We sat under a small tree on the edge of an irrigation
pond that gurgled with the water which sustained
the barley fields around us.

Every fifteen minutes, a young monk trotted out
of the monastery to refill our cups with salty butter
tea. I took the required sip, which is expected by
tradition, but after the monk left, I unmercifully
watered the barley crop with the rest of the tea.

45. **Altar in Samye Monastery, Central Tibet:** Drawn on location. 1988. Sepia ink on 11" x 14" archival paper.

During a three-day stay at Samye Monastery, John Westmore and I were invited into a private shrine-room by a young monk who guarded the doorway, so we would have an hour of quiet and meditative time to draw. The inside of monasteries and shrine-rooms are usually dimly lit or crowded with pilgrims filing through, which makes it difficult to get an unobstructed view. Private altars are always more interesting than the larger monastic altars, because they are less formal and have an ambience that reflects the monk or lama who created them. This is one of the few personal altars that I have drawn.

Samye Monastery, Tibet
Monks Altar

Changtang #5 Kailash, Tibet

Changtang #1

46. **Changtang Plateau Series:** Graphite on 5" x 23" archival paper.

The vast expanse of the Changtang Plateau in West Tibet is in complete contrast to the surrounding landscape. After spending weeks in the vertical world of the Himalayas, which form the Changtang's southern border, the horizontal character of western Tibet is overwhelming. In the higher areas of the Changtang, one can see a slight curvature in the surface of the earth. These above studies were drawn with a 9-B carpenter's pencil and attempt to reflect that horizontal character.

One problem I had while drawing there stemmed from being above a third of the earth's atmosphere where the bright ultraviolet light burns

the skin and cracks the lips. Light also reflects off of bright surfaces, like the walls of monasteries, making the effort to draw a challenge. Glacier glasses make it difficult to see detail in dark areas of the subject, so my optometrist created a pair of lightweight progressive bifocals with clip-on sunglasses, which are not quite as dark as the glacier glasses.

#1 in the collection of Carole Elchert, Findlay, Ohio
#2 in the collection of Michelle and Mark Ball, Ojai, California

47. **The Wind of Liberation #4:** Sepia ink on 37" x 48" hand-made Himalayan Daphne paper.

There is a journal entry in the introduction that describes this work in detail. I changed the format of this piece by tilting the paper onto its corners, which represents what happens to prayer flags in nature. The wind twists and tatters them, and after a short period of time, the flags become weathered and tangled. Daphne paper, which is handmade in the Himalayas, is used in the monasteries for woodblock prints and for smaller prayer flags.

In one village where the paper was being made, I had to hire a porter to carry a bundle of 500 sheets down the mountain to the road, so we could get it back to Kathmandu. To my amusement, it costs more to ship the paper back to the U.S. than to purchase it and have it carried out.

In the collection of George Dewey, Victoria, Texas

48. **House in Samar, Mustang:** Drawn on location. 1998.
   Sepia ink on 11" x 14" archival paper.

   Our little expedition followed the trail under this house and into the village of Samar. While the cooks prepared our dinner in a nearby inn, I climbed over an adjoining wall into an empty horse stall and began this drawing. An elderly man came out of a door on the second floor of the home, climbed down the stones and into the corral to see what I was doing. After viewing the drawing, he invited me into the building, which houses a five-foot prayer wheel.

   When one enters or leaves the village, one is blessed by passing under thousands of prayers, which are woodblock printed onto rolls of paper that fill the cavity of the huge drum. With each rotation of the wheel, the prayers drift into the heavens and endow the pilgrim or traveler with spiritual merit.

In the collection of Mark and Tina Granville, Findlay, Ohio

SAMAR MONASTERY
MUSTANG, NEPAL

P. Sugden 98

49. **Nomadic Encampment, Western Tibet:** Drawn on location.
1996. Sepia ink on 11" x 14" archival paper.

After a circuit of the sacred Mt. Kailas, I sketched this during our last days in the old kingdom of Guge, now part of western Tibet. I am so glad that the final drawing of the trip was this sketch of a nomadic encampment, because not a day passed without our visiting the nomads or being visited by them at our camp. On that evening, ferocious Tibetan mastiffs howled at us from the nomads' encampment. To add to the distraction and merriment, a small contingent of children hovered over us while we worked, pointing and giggling at the images as they took shape. Drawing was magic for them, and their playfulness worked magic on us.

In the collection of William Hale, Lawrence, Kansas

Nomadic Encampment, Western Tibet

50. **Manuscripts on the Theory of a Unified Field:** 1998. Sepia ink and gouache on 30" x 90" Mexican bark paper.

This work was inspired by the unified field theory, an unproven idea that describes the most fundamental level of elementary particles and forces as a single, self-interacting field. Since the unified field represents the most basic, unchanging character of nature, it could also be compared to the boundless state of pure consciousness. The ancient scriptures of India refer to this state

as *Atman*, or pure self-interaction, that is, consciousness aware of itself without any external references. This work uses one of the formulas from a contemporary theory of physics and presents it as an ancient, enigmatic document.

51. **Spituk Monastery, Ladakh:** Drawn on location. 1988.
    Sepia ink on 11" x 14" archival paper.

Carole Elchert and I were in Ladakh during the winter of 1988, when I first saw Spituk from this vantage point. It is extremely cold in February, however, and I could only plan to do the sketch on a return trip in the late spring.

I decided to execute the drawing in a manner similar to the way the Hudson River artists of the late nineteenth and early twentieth centuries handled the oil sketches they created on location in such places as the Andes and the Rockies. The painters of the Hudson River School, including Thomas Cole, Edwin Church, and Albert Bierstadt, tended to exaggerate some of the natural elements-- for instance, the height of the mountains and the menace of storm clouds--to give a visionary quality to the scene.

In the collection of the Zanesville Arts Center,
Zanesville, Ohio

SHTUK MONASTERY
LADAKH
P. SVERTON

52. **Ancient Iron Soup Cauldrons, Drepung Monastery, Tibet:**
Drawn on location. 1988. Sepia ink on 11" x 14" archival
paper.

Since the 1400s, these huge soup cauldrons have
been used to prepare the tea and soups that served
thousands of monks at Drepung Monastery every
day. After the monastery was ransacked during the
Cultural Revolution, the cauldrons sat unused for
many years and fell into disrepair.

While they waited for the caretaker to unlock the
doors of the main prayer chapel, a group of Tibetan
pilgrims sat quietly, watching us draw these ancient
kettles.

In the collection of Jerry and Sally Vossler, Findlay, Ohio

53. **The Last Dance at Drigung Dundro:**
1992. Sepia ink on
48" x 72" Stonehenge archival paper.

This was the first studio work completed after I returned from Tibet in 1992. With a group of artists, I had visited Drigung Monastery several times in the past and was on friendly terms with the monks. On that trip we were invited to watch and photograph a sky burial. Halfway through the ceremony, I became a participant; the *rogyapa* (funeral butchers) allowed me to slap a piece of rope to keep the vultures back until the body was filleted and dragged onto the rocks, where it would be consumed. I was able to stand directly beside the butchers during most of the cutting and flaying process.

For the rest of the trip, images revisited my mind continually. Most of my thoughts revolved around the temporal nature of life: how one is a conscious, living being at one moment, and the very next moment, no more than a memory.

In the studio, I dealt with the experience as directly as possible. The central drawing shows the body wrapped in cloth and standing vertically to represent the life-force that stays after death. The figure on the right cuts away ignorance with a ritual dagger, while the form on the left is a cemetery dancer. Symbolizing the illusory dance of life and death, the two side figures are monks dressed in the costume usually worn in monastic dances.

54. **Birenthanti, Central Nepal:** Drawn on location. 1983. Sepia ink on 11" x 14" archival paper.

This was one of the first regions of the Himalayas in which I was able to trek. In 1978, however, there was no road here as there is today. It took two days of walking along a ridge to reach this village. On several occasions we stayed in Birenthanti for many days because the village is so irresistibly beautiful in its riverside setting.

This scene shows one of the Hindu temples situated on the main route through the village. Around a curve, a porter walks toward the viewer, carrying a heavy load of supplies, having yet to cross ranges in the Annapurna Himalayas to villages beyond.

In the collection of Richard and Beth Flowers, Findlay, Ohio

Homestead of Merchant.
Himachal Pradesh.

55. **Potala Palace, Lhasa, Tibet:** Drawn on location. 1988. Sepia ink on 11" x 14" archival paper.

The Potala Palace, the winter residence of the Dalai Lamas, is unquestionably the most photographed building in Tibet, usually from the front. Though a frontal view is certainly impressive, the angle that is atypical was the one I sought.

I walked halfway around the Potala before deciding on this perspective with the palace partly hidden by the hill on which it is built. I drew from a quiet, shady location behind a small tea stall just off the main road.

In the collection of His Holiness the Dalai Lama, Dharamsala, India

56. **Kathmandu with Satellite Dishes:** Drawn on location. 1995. Sepia ink on 11" x 14" archival paper.

The Kathmandu Guest House has been our home away from home since 1978. It was one of the first guest houses in the Thamel district of Kathmandu. At the end of our Mustang journey, I set up a studio in a large garden room and also completed some of the drawings from the rooftop of the guest house, which overlooks the city.

It was raining the day I drew this, so I sat on the roof under an overhang. Until the drawing was finished, I did not realize the humor in the contrast of satellite dishes and old buildings. The contrast was intensified when I added the ancient Buddhist temple, Swayambhu, on the hill in the background.

57. **The Final Frontier:** 1995. Sepia ink and gouache on
    37" x 90" handmade Himalayan Daphne paper.

This work evolved over a period of years. The title came first--inspired by the narration at the beginning of the television show, "Star Trek." In the West we consider outer space as the last part of nature to be conquered; whereas in the East, inner space (consciousness) is considered the final frontier. The heads, hands, and feet of the angels are painted in black and white gouache to represent that inner space.

The figures were modeled after the hand-carved angels hung on the Christmas tree that is assembled every year at the Metropolitan Museum of Art in New York.

In the collection of Jordis Fisher, Lima, Ohio

58. **Tidrom Nunnery, Central Tibet:** Drawn on location. 1991.
Sepia ink on 11" x 14" archival paper.

After days of bouncing in the jeep across the plateau and hours of strenuous walking on the steep pilgrimage trail, I decided that floating on my back in the hot sulfur springs at Tidrom Ani Gompa was the most satisfying of spiritual experiences. The nunnery--a small village situated in a stunning valley surrounded by mountains--is a pleasant location to spend time drawing. Even though a huge mastiff sunk its teeth into the back of my leg during that visit, I was still able to create as many drawings there as I would normally complete in Lhasa.

TERDROM NUNNERY, TIBET

P. Singleton 93

59. **Namche Bazar, Solu Kumbhu, Nepal:** Drawn on location. 1986. Sepia ink on 11" x 14" archival paper.

Namche Bazar is the main market village for the Sherpa who live in the Solu Kumbhu, part of the eastern Himalayas. Most trekkers and climbers on the way to the base of Mt. Everest spend at least two nights here, acclimatizing before moving on to higher elevations.

Sketching here is always relaxing, for I never have to walk far from the comfort of the guesthouse to find subject matter. Then, after returning to the lounge in the evening, I can sit comfortably and complete some of the drawings that I started earlier in the day.

This drawing shows the village's main *chorten* (shrine) in the bowl of the mountainside. Surrounding the shrine are some barley and potato fields, and the homes climb the ridge behind.

In the collection of Dr. & Mrs. Sprague, Findlay, Ohio

Chorten at Namche Bazar
Himalaya

60. **Jokhang Temple and Rooftops of Lhasa:** Drawn on location. 1986. Sepia ink on 11" x 14" archival paper.

My first journey to Lhasa in 1986 was electric. Foreigners had only been able to enter Tibet for several years by then, so Tibetans still tended to overwhelm us as we did them. This became a problem, particularly when I was trying to draw in public. However, they were generally respectful and quiet as I worked. They would smile and talk softly to each other, and in Tibetan say, "thank you," or "very beautiful." I think this may be due in part to the fact that, of the artists in Tibet, most are monks or nuns who paint religious scrolls (thangkas).

During one drawing session in Lhasa, a pilgrim grasped my upper arm and pressed his head against it several times. Later, our Tibetan interpreter said that because I was drawing monasteries and temples, the Tibetans considered my trip a spiritual pilgrimage and were sharing in the merit I gained. This thought gave me a new perspective on the work I was doing on trips and in the studio.

This sketch was done from the balcony of our second floor room at the Snowland Hotel in Lhasa, where we could peer across the rooftops of homes to the front of the Jokhang Temple, the holiest cathedral for Tibetan Buddhists.

In the collection of Jean Graham, Beaver Creek, Colorado

P. Sugden © 86   JOKHANG TEMPLE
LHASA, TIBET

61. **Order out of Chaos #1:** 1996. Sepia ink and gouache on 72" x 72" Mexican bark paper.

In the process of pulling paper out of a large metal drawer, I gently dropped sheets that drifted onto the hardwood floor of my studio. My challenge was to create an image that could pull the disarray together.

For that purpose, the *mandala* (sacred circle) came to mind. The outer borders are the traditional design found in Tibetan thangkas. The area inside the circular border shows a small temple with the roots and limbs of a pipal tree covering its walls. I positioned the mandala on the paper in a manner that would create a symbolic doorway into the main body of the work.

In the collection of Joan and Cliff Browne, Findlay, Ohio

62. **Entering the Mandala:** Sepia ink and gouache on 48" x 72" Stonehenge paper.

Usually it is the metaphysical elements of Tibetan Buddhism--particularly the concepts of perception and emptiness--that inspire my studio work. This is one of the few works in which I have incorporated some traditional elements of Tibetan art, such as the mandala and the shapes of clouds typically used in thangka paintings. I realize that the mandala is an important form, not just in Tibetan art but in many world traditions. The circle is one of those archetypal shapes that exists in our collective unconscious. As a symbol of wholeness, the circle assists in the transformation of the mind from a state of chaos to a sense of unity by acting as a visual mantra or vehicle. By using traditional elements, I am able to keep a strong connection with the central goal of Buddhist art, which is spiritual transformation.

In this work, the Nepali porter carries Buddhist prayer stones and receives spiritual merit; as he labors up the steep Himalayan trails, he symbolically enters the mandala, the spiritual cosmos. The landscape outside of the sacred circle represents the world of relative existence.

In the collection of the Brown-Forman Corporation, Louisville, Kentucky

63. **Haystacks in Pokhara, Nepal:** Drawn on location. 1983.
Sepia ink on 11" x 14" archival paper.

While I was drawing, a young boy came out of the house next to the haystacks and watched me. He sat on a wooden fence next to me without saying a word. This was surprising for such a young child, since the Nepali children are usually quite playful.

When I completed the drawing, he told me in English that he lived there and that the haystacks were used to feed their goats and cows. The stacks are pointed upward, which allows the monsoon rain to run off without ruining the hay. The cattle sometimes find shelter from the constant monsoon rains under these stacks.

After I returned home, I sent the young boy a print of the drawing.

64. **Relief Sculptures at Chongye, Yarlung Region, Tibet:**
Drawn on location. 1988. Sepia ink on 11" x 14" archival paper.

During the Cultural Revolution, this monastery, Rewa Dechen, was almost completely destroyed, and its monks either were killed or escaped. When we were there in 1988, only a handful of older monks had returned to help rebuild the main prayer chapel. Having just finished a prayer ceremony, six monks entered the courtyard and quietly watched as I completed the sketch.

The drawing shows three relief sculptures set precariously on a shelf. The larger of the three-- Chenrezig, the god of compassion--survived the devastation of the revolution.

In the collection of Nan and Frank Guglielmi, Findlay, Ohio

Riwo Dechen Monastery, Tibet

65. **Lamayuru Monastery and Cliffs, Ladakh:** Drawn on
location. 1993. Sepia ink on 11" x 14" archival paper.

I sat below the village, on the edge of the river,
to create this drawing. Opposite the river, a wall of
rock rises that is part of the mountain chain which
borders Zanskar. From there I was getting the most
distant view possible from below the cliffs of
Lamayuru Monastery.

A middle-aged shepherd sat with me while I
sketched. We had a friendly conversation about his
life in the village. It was one of those warm, pastoral
days when I might have fallen asleep, had it not been
for the conversation.

In the collection of Matthew Rejmaniak, Houston, Texas

LAMAYURU MONASTRY, LADAKH

66. Sugden drawing in Tibet. *Photo credit: Carole Elchert*

67. **A Holy Man's Cave, Changtang Plateau, Western Tibet:** 1991. Graphite on 10" x 20" archival paper.

Recently, I have been focusing on my subjective response to subject matter. An obvious example is found in the way I reacted to this cliff and cave. While working on the drawing, I noticed that if I stood closer to the subject, the forms would become less recognizable and seemingly more abstract.

In this work I used soft graphite rather than ink, as the rock is gray, but even more so to create a wider latitude of value in the drawing itself.

In the collection of Philip Gardner, Findlay, Ohio

68. **Tibetan Buddhist Mani Stones, Ladakh:** Drawn on
location. 1988. Sepia ink on 11" x 14" archival paper.

This is the southern end of the longest *mani*
(prayer) wall in Ladakh. Built along the side of the
main road leading from the capital of Leh to the
Tibetan refugee community at Choglamsar, the wall
of prayer stones is a blessing to passing travelers and
pilgrims, offering them protection from harmful
spirits or negative forces.

In Choglamsar, Carole and I were accepted and
treated as family by Tibetan refugees Jamyang
Keyma and Karma Tenphal as we worked on our
first book, *White Lotus*. Due in large part to the
hospitality and generosity of most Tibetans, I was
able to complete over 130 drawings in the refugee
settlements throughout India, Nepal, and Tibet.

In the collection of Elizabeth Beach, Fostoria, Ohio

69. **Tibetan with Prayer Beads:** Drawn on location. 1988.
Sepia ink on 8" x 10" archival paper.

During our stay at the Choglamsar Tibetan refugee settlement in Ladakh, John Westmore and I created many quick gestural drawings like this one, which took only seconds to produce. I filled a small sketchbook with this kind of work during a political rally in the crowded parade field of the camp.

In the collection of Jeanie and Steve Gillen, Findlay, Ohio